by Ryan Harrold
illustrated by Doreen Gay-Kassel

Printed in China

ISBN 10: 0-15-350683-0
ISBN 13: 978-0-15-350683-3

Ordering Options
ISBN 10: 0-15-350600-8 (Grade 3 On-Level Collection)
ISBN 13: 978-0-15-350600-0 (Grade 3 On-Level Collection)
ISBN 10: 0-15-357904-8 (package of 5)
ISBN 13: 978-0-15-357904-2 (package of 5)

2 3 4 5 6 7 8 9 10 985 12 11 10 09 08 07

Characters

Jordan **Ellen** **Sharon** **Max** **Jack**

Setting: A street being used as a film set

Jordan: We're coming to you today from the set of the film *Lunch Break*.

Sharon: *Lunch Break* will be filmed at a number of locations around town for the next few weeks. We're lucky to have some of the people involved in the film here today to talk about what they do. Welcome, everybody!

Jack: Thank you. We're delighted to be here.

Jordan: That's Jack Park, the director of the film.

Sharon: Jack, how did you get involved in filmmaking?

Jack: I always loved telling stories. First, I made storybooks. Then my family got a video camera. I couldn't put it down! I made an enormous number of movies starring people in my neighborhood.

Jordan: Did you study filmmaking in school?

Jack: Yes, in college. Afterward, though, I had all kinds of jobs on film sets. I watched other directors work. I learned a lot that way.

Sharon: What exactly does a director do?

Jack: Directors decide the best way to tell the story in the script. They decide how each scene will look. They help the actors perform. They help choose sound effects and music. They're really responsible for the whole film.

Jordan: That's quite a burden for one person!

Jack: That's why it's mandatory that you put together a crew of talented people to help you!

Jordan: Is that the first thing you do when you're going to make a film?

Jack: There's a lot to do before you start filming. Choosing a crew is important. You also have to decide where to film. Sometimes you build sets inside a studio. Sometimes you need to go outside to find the right place. For example, a friend suggested Bloomfield for *Lunch Break*. I came to visit, and it was perfect!

Sharon: We're glad you're here.

Jack: I am, too. Then I break the script down into tiny pieces. I draw a picture to show how I want each scene to look. These are called storyboards. They look like panels in a comic strip. I show them to people, and we plan how we're going to film them. We think about what we'll need. The director of photography plays an important part here.

Jordan: Ellen, you're the director of photography. Please tell us what you do.

Ellen: Sure. I'm in charge of the cameras and lights. I choose the type of film to use to get the right look. I talk with the director about how to film each shot. I'm also in charge of lighting.

Sharon: I've noticed there are a lot of lights around here!

Ellen: Light helps the mood of a scene. Lighting can make an actor look bold and heroic. It can make a quiet scene look tender and warm.

Jordan: What's a day on the set like?

Jack: It's long! The crew comes to the location early. They have to make sure everything we need is there. Ellen's lighting crew works on setting up the lights. The actors come early, too. They need to get into their costumes and makeup. Max is our makeup artist.

Sharon: I guess Max is the one who makes movie stars look so glorious!

Max: That's only part of it. Movie actors really need makeup. The lights are very bright. Without makeup, they would look quite dull. I also do effects with makeup. I can make someone young look old. I can make someone look bald without cutting his hair. I can create monsters. I can make someone who is healthy look sick.

Jordan: That must take a long time!

Max: Sometimes makeup can take hours. Actors have to be patient.

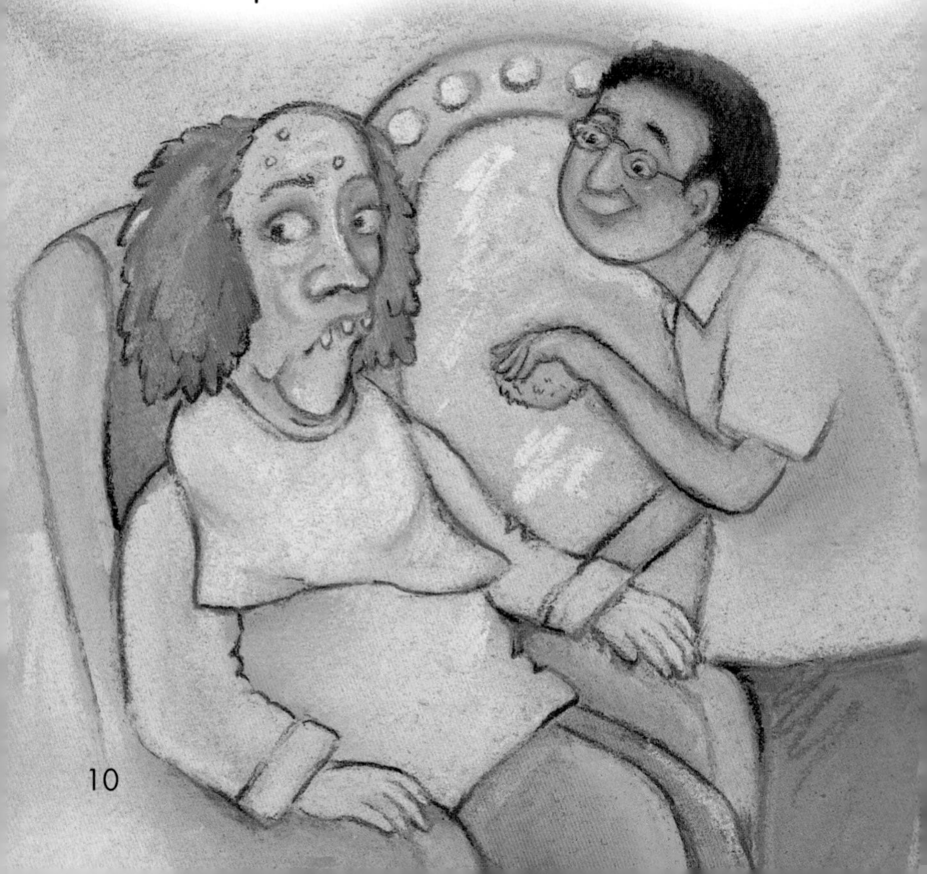

Sharon: Jack, when do you rehearse the scenes with the actors?

Jack: We don't rehearse much. Film actors really need to prepare on their own. They have to immerse themselves in the script. Some may work on the dialogue with a coach. You don't want a good scene ruined because someone forgets a line! Then when the actors get on the set, I'll give them some direction. We'll run through it. Then we'll shoot the scene.

Jordan: Isn't that hard?

Jack: Film scenes are short. That makes it easy to give direction and make changes. It helps to have good actors, though!

Sharon: How many script pages do you film each day?

Jack: It's a good day if we film three pages.

Jordan: That's all?

Jack: Absolutely. We film the same scene many times. We film from different angles and distances. Then when the whole script has been filmed, we edit together the best versions.

Sharon: It sounds like there is a lot to do after you finish filming.

Jack: Right. You need to edit all the film. You need to add sound effects and special effects. You add music. There's a lot to do!

Jordan: It sounds very complicated! What would you tell people interested in becoming filmmakers?

Jack: I'd say be creative and try different things. Some may work. Some may not. Listen if people criticize your work. You may learn something.

Ellen: I'd remind people that there are a lot of different jobs in movies. Just think about how long the credits are after a movie! Each of those people had some effect on it. You could be an actor or director. However, you could also be a director of photography or an editor.

Max: You could become a makeup artist or a costume designer.

Sharon: It sounds like there's something for almost everyone. Thanks for talking to us!

Jordan: We can't wait to see *Lunch Break*!

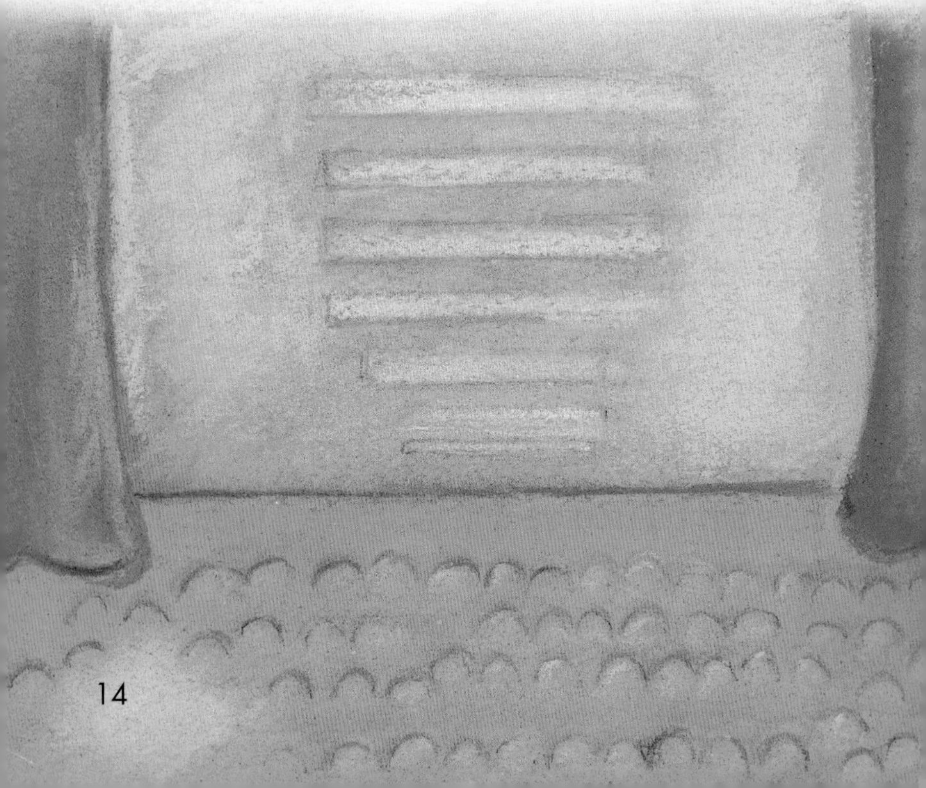

Think Critically

1. How is filming a movie different than putting on a play?

2. What is the theme of this Readers' Theater?

3. Why are so few pages of a script filmed each day?

4. What does a director have to do before filming begins?

5. Which of the jobs described in this Readers' Theater sounds the most interesting to you? Why?

Drama

Film It! Think of a book you like. Imagine that it is being made into a movie. Write a scene from the book as you would like to see it in the movie. Ask classmates to help you read the parts.

School-Home Connection Ask family members about their favorite movies and share your favorites as well. Discuss why you liked these movies.

Word Count: 940